Hinckley

in old picture postcards

by
Frank Shaw

European Library - Zaltbommel/Netherlands MCMLXXXVII

GB   ISBN 90 288 4535 6 / CIP

© 1987 European Library - Zaltbommel/Netherlands

European Library in Zaltbommel/Netherlands publishes among other things the following series:

IN OLD PICTURE POSTCARDS *is a series of books which sets out to show what a particular place looked like and what life was like in Victorian and Edwardian times. A book about virtually every town in the United Kingdom is to be published in this series. By the end of this year about 300 different volumes will have appeared. 1,500 books have already been published devoted to the Netherlands with the title* **In oude ansichten.** *In Germany, Austria and Switzerland 650, 100 and 25 books have been published as* **In alten Ansichten;** *in France by the name* **En cartes postales anciennes** *and in Belgium as* **In oude prentkaarten** *and/or* **En cartes postales anciennes** *150 respectively 400 volumes have been published.*

For further particulars about published or forthcoming books, apply to your bookseller or direct to the publisher.

This edition has been printed and bound by Grafisch Bedrijf De Steigerpoort in Zaltbommel/Netherlands.

INTRODUCTION

It would take a book many times larger than this to give a full history of Hinckley. This book simply shows how people lived, dressed and worked and how Hinckley looked between 1880 and 1930. For much of the information contained in the footnotes to each photograph I am indebted to Gregory Drozdz, who has given willingly of both his time and knowledge.

Hinckley holds a rather unique position in British history. When the very first Baron of Hinckley was appointed by William the Conquerer, he was also made hereditary Lord High Steward of England. Fifteen successive Lords of Hinckley held the office of Lord High Steward, of whom one was Henry of Bolingbroke, Duke of Lancaster and Baron of Hinckley. In 1399 he was crowned King Henry IV.

So great had become the power of the Lord High Steward that after the Coronation of Henry IV, no further permanent appointment was ever made to that office. A temporary appointment only has been made since that time and even that appointment has been for just two special purposes. The first purpose is the arraignment or charging of a Peer to the Realm for a capital crime. The second purpose is to officiate at a Coronation. On Coronation day the Lord High Steward walks immediately before the Sovereign bearing St. Edward's Crown.

Hinckley is also the home of the Hosiery Trade following the introduction of the first stocking frame into the town by William Iliffe prior to 1640. There is little doubt that William Iliffe was also a native of the town for the name appears frequently in the Registers. In 1649 he married Elizabeth Cleveland, daughter of the Vicar of Hinckley.

In 1722 Robert Atkins, then aged 20, was released from his Apprenticeship Indentures and so was then free to make stockings on his own account. He started in business and from that small beginning has grown the business now known as 'Atkins of Hinckley' which still operates in the town. It is now the oldest existing and operating commercial company in the world. Robert Atkins, its founder, died in 1768 and is buried at Hinckley.

When he came to Hinckley in 1722 it consisted of a small township of just over 2,000 inhabitants – about 350 families in total. But William Iliffe's stocking frame had revolutionised the hosiery trade and by 1778 there were no fewer than 864 frames in the town. Most were confined to cottages but the trade was still increasing rapidly.

The reader can then perhaps understand the nature of Hinckley's subscription for the British troops under the Duke of York serving on the continent in the Napoleonic Wars. It was a subscription made in the winter of 1793 and took the form of 2,800 pairs of 'good strong serviceable worsted stockings' and '70 flannel waistcoats'. Each to his trade! But it was a substantial gift from what was still a small town.

Their reward came with the conclusion of peace with France in 1802. On 1st April that year fourteen sheep were roasted in the streets of Hinckley 'for the rejoicing'.

In 1831 the sum of £131.46 was raised by subscription to celebrate the Coronation of William IV of which one third was spent on beer! The following distribution was made to each person: ten ounces of meat, half a pound of bread and one pound of potatoes. In addition each adult received one pint of ale with half a pint to children under twelve years of age!

In 1835 there was designed, constructed and developed in Hinckley the original Hansom Cab. It was first tested along Coventry Road, Hinckley, by Joseph Aloysius Hansom, resident of the town, and despite the general laughter at its then unique appearance, it went on to become a symbol of the Victorian London of foggy streets and Sherlock Holmes!

However, by 1867 there was a general dissatisfaction with the way the town was being governed and a meeting of townspeople decided that the town ought to be governed by a Local Board. Elections took place in February 1868 and the power of Local Government, including the Fire Brigade and the Cemetery, was transferred to the new Local Government Board.

The first job to be tackled was the provision of a proper water supply but it seems every member had his own pet scheme and it was not until twenty-three years and six Consulting Engineers later that a piped supply came to Hinckley. Times now are not so different after all!

However, in fairness to the Board, in 1871 it did acquire land for a recreation ground. That has now become Queens Park. In 1875 it established the Sewage Disposal Works at Sketchley Farm. It also bought property, demolished it and so widened Station Road to what it is today. Local historians however regard its career as somewhat chequered – and stormy!

The Hinckley Urban District Council came into being on 31st December 1894. The town by now had a population of about 10,000. But it had no electricity, cinema, dance hall or motorised transport. The first motor car passed through Hinckley in 1898. However, it clearly had public houses that were well-supported, for the first Urban Council of fifteen members was comprised of nine 'Liberals', four 'Conservatives' and two 'Licensed Victuallers'!

Electricity was introduced to the town in 1912 by which time the population was 13,000. But further progress stopped with the Great War of 1914-1918.

Several families of Belgian war refugees were accommodated in Hinckley in this period and the Council agreed to supply gas free of charge to them and to remit all rates.

The Urban District Council also passed a resolution in 1916 that was somewhat ahead of its time – fifty-five years to be exact! On 17th October 1916 it was resolved that, 'the Council consider it not only desirable but absolutely essential to adopt the decimal system of coinage, weights and measures throughout the British Isles and thus compete more easily and successfully with rival nations having that system already in use'.

But the Great War had cost Hinckley dear – as it did all the cities, towns and villages. The names of 384 dead from Hinckley alone are recorded on the War Memorial in Argents Mead.

After the Armistice, a major programme of redevelopment involving new building on open land and the replacing of many older dwellings took place. In one year, 1919, thirty-seven acres of land was acquired by the Council for housing purposes and that pace was maintained. Today Hinckley has changed out of all recognition of those days, as these photographs show. We believe it is a pleasant town with a friendly population.

But why not come and see for yourself?

Frank Shaw
Principal Chief Officer and
Director of Administration & Finance
Hinckley & Bosworth Borough Council.

1. John Street in the 1920's, as viewed from the junction with Leicester Road. The dwellings on either side to the junction with Highfields Road still remain but today the rest of the street is one of contrasts. The other end, nearest to Derby Road, is now almost exclusively factories. At the turn of the century John Street formed the town limits and one had to walk across a field to get to Leicester Road.

2. May 20th, 1910 at the junction of Market Place and Castle Street. The well-respected tailoring concern of W. Gilder is shuttered for the memorial service of the late King Edward VII. Members of the Hinckley Urban District Council, the Magistrates and the Board of Guardians make their way through a crowded Market Place to the service at St. Mary's Church. A thousand tickets for the service had been issued and they had all been taken within two days.

UPPER CASTLE STREET, HINCKLEY

3. Upper Castle Street about 1911 looking down towards New Buildings. The shapes of the shop windows, then belonging to Chamberlain's and Gould's, have hardly altered and the view is easily recognisable today.

4. The Market Place as it existed for our older residents. Simpkin and James were a well-known local grocery concern and no doubt the aromas from the ground coffee beans and the tea leaves drew in many a customer. You could hire a carriage for a funeral or a wedding from the George Inn – always an enterprising hostelry!

Hollycroft, Hinckley

5. Known in former times as Hollow Croft, this view of Hollycroft taken about 1910 shows the large town houses. They fronted on to Hollycroft Park, opened in 1935. The land formerly belonged to the Atkins family. The hill looks far less steep than it actually is.

Castle Street, Hinckley

6. Instantly recognisable to locals as Castle Street. The shop awnings create a beautiful atmosphere of enclosure and security. The 'Victoria Inn' is in the right foreground. The large house behind the shop on the left was once occupied by Hinckley's authoress Charlotte Brame. She died there on 28th November 1884.

7. The junction of Spa Lane and London Road in 1913. Children play on the green whilst a tradesman, with his horse and cart, makes a house call. One man has taken the opportunity to sit down on his wheelbarrow and have a rest! The tree in the middle of the green was planted in 1887 to commemorate Queen Victoria's Jubilee. The green remains, but children could not be left to play on it now as they do in this picture.

8. Orchard Street as seen from Hill Street in the early 1900's. Today, the private house on the corner, to the right in the photograph, has lost its railed seclusion and fronts directly onto Orchard Street which otherwise had hardly changed.

9. Castle Street about 1923. Allsopp's Pork Butchers eventually was to move onto Regent Street. This family were well-known for their pork pies and Edward Allsopp was one of the leading members of the local Salvation Army, doing much to further their cause in the town. The motor transport bears testimony to a developing Castle Street and this photograph should be compared with No. 6. It is hard to imagine that there was once heavy two-way traffic on this street.

1958 Hinckley Men of the D Squadron Lutterworth Troop Leicestershire Imperial Yeomanry, at Hinckley, May 16th, 1907.

10. May 16th, 1907. Bystanders on the cobbled pavement look on at the smartly turned out local men and horses of D Squadron, Lutterworth Troop, Leicestershire Imperial Yeomanry. The men all wear bandoliers of ammunition in the manner popularised by the Boer War. When trench warfare took its grip during the early days of the First World War the cavalry horse and cavalry charge became obsolete, although the horse played its part in the final victory. This photograph was taken shortly before the troop went off to its summer camp at Beaumanor Park.

11. The unmistakable slope of Clarendon Road about 1900. The right of the picture is a contrast with the build-up of the street today but the large houses of the well-to-do are very typical of much of the suburban development of the town. The trees are a reminder that this part of the town was once beautifully wooded and Clarendon Road was known as 'Lover's Walk'.

12. Lower Bond Street on a sunny day in a less hurried time, February 1914. Atkins factory and the Barley Sheaf Inn are still joined together today as they are in the photograph. Houses once stood where the factory complex was built in 1895, one of them being the home of the Atkins family. Troops would be soon marching over the cobbles and a particularly warm welcome was extended to a company of the Durham Fusiliers, who happened to break their march in Lower Bond Street, shortly after the war began. The Barley Sheaf is thought to be the oldest public house in the town, with vaults dating back to the 1600's.

BURBAGE ROAD, HINCKLEY

140 A

13. London Road. This view is taken from the junction with Spa Lane in 1905. The road was at various times known as Lutterworth Road and Burbage Road. Children would be well-advised not to stand there today! The trees further along from the houses on the left conceal the old workhouse, built in 1838. It was demolished in 1947 and the land used to build the extension of the Hinckley College of Further Education.

Ashby Road, Hinckley.

14. Ashby Road in 1915. The house front left is known as 'Elm-Lea' and belonged to the Davis family, who were local hosiery manufacturers. It is now used as an old people's home. Both sides of the road have now become quite heavily built up, but in 1916, the largest community was in the cemetery behind the clump of trees bottom right, known locally as 'Sparrow's Garden'.

Free Library and Council Offices, Hinckley

15. The Free Library and Council Offices in 1905. The Library building as far as the three perpendicular windows was built in 1888 by Messrs. John, Thomas and Hugh Atkins in memory of their late brother Arthur. The land had been formerly occupied by the postman's house 'who kept a fearful dog' to guard the mails and the plot was purchased from the Ecclesiastical Commissioners for £250. The building was opened by the Duchess of Rutland. The extension that was to be the Council Offices was added in 1903. The building is one of Hinckley's most enduring façades, and remains almost unchanged today.

Station Road, Hinckley.

16. Station Road looking back towards the town and the Market Place. The large houses, once residential, are now almost exclusively professional offices. The horse and cart are just passing the entrance to Mount Road. There was once open ground to the left-hand side of the road where travelling theatres and circuses would pitch their tents and stages. It was one of Hinckley's busiest roads with goods and merchandise being brought to and from the Station. Workers from other towns such as Nuneaton would come to Hinckley to work in the local hosiery factories and alighted at the Station and then made their way into the town.

17. The Lawns, 1910. Once open ground sloping gently down to the Castle and Moat some distance to the right and known as the Lawn. Is the horse and cart on the wrong side of the road? As there is no other traffic it doesn't seem to matter!

18. Derby Road, as seen from Ashby Road, showing its junction with Druid Street. The façades of the houses on the right remain much the same since this photograph was taken in 1909. Notice the full length voluminous black dress of the woman on the pavement.

Leicester Road, Hinckley

19. Leicester Road, 1918. The corner house of Highfields Road (left) is easily recognised. Over twenty small children play in a quite relaxed way at what is now a major road junction. There were several games played by children, such as 'choc-hole', 'alley' or 'grog' – all variations of marbles. Spinning tops made of wood were very popular and running a hoop with a stick of wood was good exercise! However, we seem to have two 'poseurs' on the right!

Spa Lane, Hinckley. No. 2690.

20. The houses are still with us but grass no longer grows in a much busier Spa Lane. This photograph was taken in the 1920's. The cyclist is just passing Bowling Green Road, which was not made up until the 1950's.

Priesthills Road, Hinckley. No. 2601.

21. The camber of the road has been improved but otherwise time has stood still in this photograph of Priesthills Road in 1925. A careful look towards the far distance reveals that the portion of the road connecting it with Queens Road from Hurst Road has not yet been developed as there is still a screen of trees.

A159. Highfield Road Hinckley.

22. Highfields Road from Leicester Road looking across John Street to open fields. The road takes its name from the fact that it is situated at the highest point in the town. The road is in need of a better surface but there is an air of tranquility in this photograph which contrasts with the parked cars and heavy traffic of today.

Church Walk. A bit of old Hinckley.

23. Happily caught for posterity in this photograph about 1910 are the thatched cottages which used to line Church Walk. They were demolished in the 1950's for an approach road to the car park. Debate still rages in the town as to whether these beautiful cottages should ever have been pulled down. A unique part of Hinckley and its history was lost forever to our eternal shame.

24. There are fewer trees now but these houses on the London Road, near the junction with Spa Lane, retain their same grandeur. On the opposite side of the road was the old Fire Station and later the College of Further Education.

25. The market stalls trade busily today just as when this photograph was taken in 1905. The two storied house behind the lamp-post (right) has been replaced by Lloyd's Bank and this site has seen much recent development.

Mount Road, Hinckley.

26. The horse and cart are passing the junction to Hurst Road in this 1912 photograph of Mount Road. The sweep of the road is familiar but many of the houses front right and beyond have been demolished to make way for development.

27. Although this photograph was taken in 1907, this view of Station Road could be contemporary, with the Constitutional Club and shops to the right and the National School and Library to the left.

28. Hall & Son were later to move across the road but the building is still recognisable as Pickering's (Stationers, which stood till recently) next to the present National Westminster Bank. There appears to be the vestige of a market stall. The horse may well be pulling a wagon of beer barrels as it stands in front of Everards Brewery premises. In the background is the Union Hotel.

Post Office and Station Road, Hinckley

29. The dawning of the new century – the town's first and only purpose built Post Office built in 1902 and still in use today. Opposite was to be the Billiard Hall, built by Amos Taylor of Burnley. Despite the extensive and no doubt colourful advertising hoardings on the garage, there is not a motor vehicle in sight!

THE BOROUGH, HINCKLEY.

30. The Borough, about 1930. The Hinckley bus, looking like a railway coach placed on a vehicle chassis, makes its way towards Regent Street and Hunt's mineral water van makes a delivery. The building behind the bus has long since been demolished – first for an extension of the Market Place and more lately professional offices and a bank.

Cottage Hospital, Hinckley.

5

31. Hinckley's first Cottage Hospital was in Wood Street in 1890. It was then moved to Hill Street but with increasing demands upon the already stretched resources, land was bought on Mount Road to commemorate Queen Victoria's Diamond Jubilee. Such were the efforts of local people that the building in this photograph was ready for opening by late 1900. The uniforms have altered but the portals of the Cottage Hospital remain the same today. The local building firm of Jeffcote, still in existence, were the contractors involved in the building of the hospital. The photograph was taken in 1912.

REGENT STREET. HINCKLEY

32. The buildings on the right hand side of the photograph were very typical of the many older buildings in the town – very different from the present Edwards Centre! This was the spot where Joseph Hansom developed his first 'Hansom Cab'. Regent Street today would not see such a comfortable mix of motor car and horse and cart, as in this photograph of 1920.

175 S.   STATION ROAD, HINCKLEY.

33. Station Road 1918. The children pose at the junction with Priesthills Road and Clarendon Road. The road shows signs of horse and cart use but the view of the spire of St. Mary's would today be obscured.

Hollycroft, Hinckley. No. 2694.

34. Hollycroft, 1920, and a reminder of the huge trees which dominated this side of Hollycroft Park until very recent times. Right foreground is the entrance to Factory Road. A motorbike with sidecar makes its way up the steeper part of the hill leaving the lady and her pram (also in the road) struggling behind! Hollycroft was known colloquially as 'Canning's Walk' after George Canning, Prime Minister, who lived in the town from 1807 to 1811. He would walk out of the town towards Stoke Golding and Wykin.

35. The upside down cross on the banner quickly denotes this procession in Castle Street as being that of St. Peter's School. The banner attracted much comment until it was pointed out that the cross in that position was meant to be a sign of humility. Such processions were common and the non-conformist chapels each had their own separate processions known as the 'Treats'. In recent years the churches have walked together. This photograph was taken in 1908.

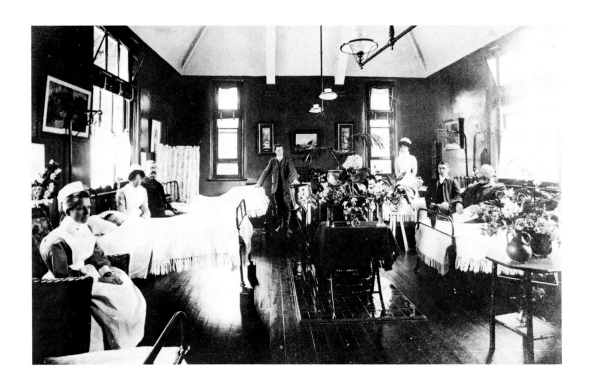

36. The interior of Hinckley Cottage Hospital, 1905. Apparently the Children's Ward with only two patients! The pride taken in the hospital is evident just from the shining polished floors. Note the gas lighting and stove in the middle of the ward.

37. No parking problems in Queens Road in 1913! It seems to be a much more relaxed street in those days. The exteriors of the houses have hardly changed.

Market Place and Borough Hinckley. 101/4.

38. The expanse of the Market Place and the rounded corner of Castle Street in 1907. They are one of the town's most prominent and enduring features. The Town Hall Arms was built in 1806 and today houses Barclays Bank. When gas lighting was first brought to the Market Place it caused quite a stir. The owner of the Market Tolls, one John Toone, would not allow the workmen to put up the standard in the middle of the Market Place and even placed a wagon over the intended spot for the lamp. Following a High Court decision in London and compensation to Mr. Toone, the lamp went up!

39. Another view of Hollycroft. The last town crier, Mr. Thomas Cassell, used to call from the top of Hollycroft and when the wind was in the right direction he could be clearly heard in Higham and Stoke Golding. Of course, the area was then open fields and the Battling Brook stream. Thomas Cassell stopped calling about 1903, when this photograph was taken. He was the great grandfather of Gregory Drozdz, who has given great assistance in compiling this book.

The Borough, Hinckley

40. Another view of the Borough, this time showing on the left the Hinckley Theatre, later the Odeon Cinema. Wightmans Sports Outfitters nestled on the ground floor behind the pillars. It has all now been demolished and today is the site of the Anglia Building Society. Hall & Son dates from 1859 and came to specialise in school uniforms. Children about to go to school for the first time or even change schools would be taken to Halls to be 'fixed-up' in the correct uniform.

41. A tranquil corner of Hinckley in 1904. Unbelievably, it is the junction of Leicester Road and New Buildings, looking along Derby Road. The home on the left is now a motor car showroom and a filling station now exists to the right of the photograph.

177 S.   THE BOROUGH, HINCKLEY.

42. The Borough, and all quiet on Hinckley's front in 1918. There appear to be some residential premises in the buildings on the left which are now all Offices and Banks. The road here was cobbled until very recently. The houses in the distance have been demolished for road widening schemes. The Borough and Bond-End retained individual identities for a very long time and still take a pride in being different from each other.

43. Another view of the thatched cottages in Church Walk in 1905. Near here lived two of the town's well-known characters, Billy Humphries, the postman, and 'Sir' William North, of the Order of Buffaloes. Humphries lived next door to a painter and decorator by the name of Fred Cassell and would use the different pieces of wallpaper from Cassell's old samplers to paper his rooms. Far from being a pot-pourri, the walls were tastefully done!

44. Regent Street about 1880 – long before modernisation reached it. The poplar trees are evidence that the area was semi-rural! Apparently the cobbled pavement exists today, albeit that it is now covered over with tarmac. The street once bore the rather quaint title of 'Duckpaddle Lane'. In the distance there is the junction with Coventry Road.

45. The terrace of houses at the top of Spa Lane were built to special designs and were much admired and sought after in their day. They have all been carefully renovated and preserved. Spa Lane takes its title from St. Christopher's Spa or Spring that emerges close to the bowling green in the road of the same name.

46. Looking up London Road towards the junction with Spa Lane. The contours of the road and the buildings are much the same today.

Hill Street, Hinckley

47. When I see this photograph I think how lucky we are to have this reminder of Hill Street in about 1920 in its prime. Virtually nothing of the original of the left hand side remains today. The houses on the left close to the photographer have only been recently demolished.

48. Hinckley United Football Club 1911-1912 complete with child 'mascot'! The club was founded in 1906 and played on the Holywell, London Road, Hinckley. The nickname was the 'Units'. Back row, left to right: W. Marshall, W. Brown, J. Thomas (Chairman), W. Webster and G. Whitmore. Middle row, left to right: H. Hewitt, W. Pinchess, J. Payne, T. Linney, G. Noon, T. Foster, J. Hancox (Secretary), A. Pick, T. King, C. Osbourne, J. Herbert, S. Marlow (trainer) and W. Gran. Front row, left to right: F. Puffer, H.W. Line, F.W. Price, A.R. Warren, E. Bee and E. Warburton. Child mascot unidentified. Despite the two trophies on display this was the worst season for the Units since their inception. The team is pictured with the Hinckley Charity Cup and the Coalville Charity Cup. Osbourne and Pick had been regulars in the side since 1906 but one wonders how many of these young men went off to fight in the war, only two years later, and how many never returned?

49. There were several bands in the town at one time, including the Town Band, the Great Meeting Band, the band of the Volunteer Corps and several others. This is a photograph of the Hinckley Military Band, which was formed by Mr. C.A. Whatmore, assisted by Mr. P.W. Powell. The aim of the band was to provide a repertoire of popular classic music and they played for dancing at outdoor events. The older looking man, seated third from the right, appears to be wearing a campaign medal and the three stripes of a sergeant.

171 S.   DERBY AVENUE, HINCKLEY.

50. Derby Avenue, now Derby Road, about 1920. The gracious house with the large wooden gate to the right is the 'Limes', formerly belonging to Marjery Payne, a town benefactoress. It is now the site of an elderly persons' home bearing the same name. On the left is the 'Weaver's Arms' which is much enhanced in appearance today and still very popular. One feels the lamp-post would not last long in the heavy traffic that now passes this spot.

51. One of the town's several tollgates in 1909. This tollgate house stood at the Burbage turn on the present Sapcote Road and was demolished in the early years of this century. There were several turnpike roads leading out of the town, each with its tollgate. They were situated on the Ashby Road nearly opposite Barwell Lane, on Leicester Road near to the lane leading to Burbage Common, on the Rugby Road at the foot of Sketchley Hill and on the Coventry Road near to Clarendon Fields. The tollgate house in this photograph would have seen all the London traffic approaching the town, which would have been considerable as Hinckley grew in importance in relation to the hosiery trade. The photograph was given to me by Mrs. Spencer of Barrie Road who is the baby being carried in the picture!

52. Lower Bond Street about 1910. The old Manor House, which is now the Police Station, belonged to Thomas Sansome, and can be seen behind the trees in the distance. The houses on the right have completely disappeared to make way for extensions to Atkins Factory. The Hollybush Inn, on the site of an old horsepool, stands on the corner opposite the present Police Station. On the far right was the entrance to 'Cuckoo's alley'.

53. The sign on the corner of this building says 'To the Railway Station' and this is the site of the present Midland Bank premises in the Market Place. The cobbled pavement is known as the 'petrified kidney' pavement. This building, symptomatic of the state of desrepair of many of the town's older buildings, had the rather dignified title of Queens Court. It jutted out into Station Road and was demolished when that road and the entrance to the market needed to be widened to cope with heavier traffic. Part of the land was sold to the Leicestershire Banking Company at 21/- a yard. Older residents may well remember the London, City and Midland Bank on this site. On the far right can be seen one of the twelve public water pumps in the town.

54. Then as now, the store with the latest in household fittings and gardening equipment. When this photograph was taken at the turn of the century they were advertising 'Robertsons Lamps'. The concern regularly won prizes at the Leicestershire Agricultural Show for having the most modern equipment on sale. Now Charles Corts, it is still known locally as 'Parsons Sherwin'.

55. St. Mary's Church, the town's oldest architectural inheritance, has seen all the changes in the Market Place, where Hinckley's citizens have thronged to their Monday market since 1550. If one compares the junction of Station Road and the Market Place with photograph 53 one can see the improvements that have been made. The old Globe Inn is still standing though, where Church Walk meets Station Road when this photograph was taken. It was demolished in 1905 but in its day it was famous for its tripe suppers.

56. The frontage onto the Market Place where the Town and Country Building Society offices are situated. This particular frontage has seen many changes, from a public house to a furniture and electrical goods shop, to insurance offices and a travel agents, amongst others.

57. This was the Bull's Head Tavern, one of the principal hostelries in the town, with over thirty rooms for lodgings and stabling for a hundred horses or more. At one time it was the repository for the local mails. Ann Bass was the proprietor for a good number of years. It fronted onto Market Place and part of it can be seen in photograph 56.

58. The disappearance of the cottages in Church Walk through neglect might also have been the fate of the well-loved Framework Knitters' Cottages but for the intervention of Atkins Bros., who purchased and restored the property. Judging by this 1920's photograph, it was obviously even then in state of decay. Reputedly built about 1720, the cottages were once a farm house. In the Hinckley Times and Bosworth Herald of July 1896, there is recorded, in the local dialect, the story of Andrew Goode, a stockinger. It begins: *Old Andrew Goode wer one of the old fashioned sort o' stockingers; 'im and 'ss wife live in one o' them little thack 'ousin up Bond End; Wick arter wick Andrew sot in 's old frame from early morn tell bedtime. No matter when yer went past the dure, yer wer certin t' hear 'im gooing at it – sheet-a-boom-boom-cr-r-r-r-, allus the same old rattle. They was nivver onny too well off, they wasn't, and as they got older they kep a gettin wusser off all the time astid o' better.*

CORONATION OF GEORGE ... FESTIVITIES AT HINCKLEY, JUNE 1911

59. Thursday, 22nd June 1911. This photograph shows the children's procession coming up Castle Street, as part of a three day programme of festivities to celebrate the Coronation of George V. The procession started in the Borough and by way of Castle Street, Grimm's Lane (New Buildings), Derby Road, and Bond Street, returned to the Borough, to then sing patriotic songs. In the procession were 2,800 school children, drawn from both Day and Sunday schools. They dispersed to their respective schoolrooms to be given tea and sandwiches and then a coronation mug as a souvenir of the occasion.

60. Trinity Lane about 1900. The corner shop and the terraced houses still stand today but the opposite side of the road has given way to warehouses. The shop is on the corner of Mill Hill Road and Trinity Lane. The much narrower entrance to Mansion Street is in the middle of the left-hand side.

61. The Blue Boar gives us a clue to this very old photograph of Regent Street. This picture shows the felling of the last poplar tree, once a familiar local landmark, to make way for building developments. Some may remember White's Garage on this site before Atkins purchased the site for their factory, built in 1930-31. Shop premises were also built as part of the complex and today form the Regent Arcade. Regent Street was something of a town boundary. Those on the Coventry Road side of it were known as the downtowners. Those on the other side were known as the uptowners. A phrase still used in the town is 'I'm gooing uptown'.

22291 PARISH CHURCH. HINCKLEY.

62. After the Norman conquest of the Britain the original Church and Abbey were erected in Hinckley in 1097. Nothing of the Abbey remains, although it is possible that there are some foundations left under the houses and carpark on St. Mary's Road. The church was rebuilt in the 14th century, coming to look much as it does today. The National School in the foreground, now St. Mary's Primary School, bears testimony to the influence of the Church on education.

63. The warehouse of Wykes & Son in Regent Street for their fruit and vegetable business. Many will remember their last one in George Street, now the site of the Chinese Restaurant.

Castle Street, Hinckley

64. Castle Street in 1912. The contours are much the same and it is doubtful whether the word 'pedestrianisation' had entered the language then. There were many local businessmen driving horses and carts and selling their wares directly to the public from their drays. Mr. Ernie 'Bunny' Ayres sold tripe and the sound of his bell would send the children scurrying to purchase six pennyworth of tripe and a jug of gravy for their mothers. There was also a water cart, needed because of problems with the town's water supply and the 'Nine O'Clock Horses' were the carts that came to take away the sewage from people's backyards.

65. The class of 1870! These privileged boys attended the school at the Drill Hall on Grimm's Lane, later New Buildings. There were a number of schools in the town but educational opportunities were still limited. The school at the Drill Hall later became the Grammar School. James Wykes of Wykes & Son (see photographs 63 and 67) is somewhere amongst the scholars – unfortunately he cannot be identified.

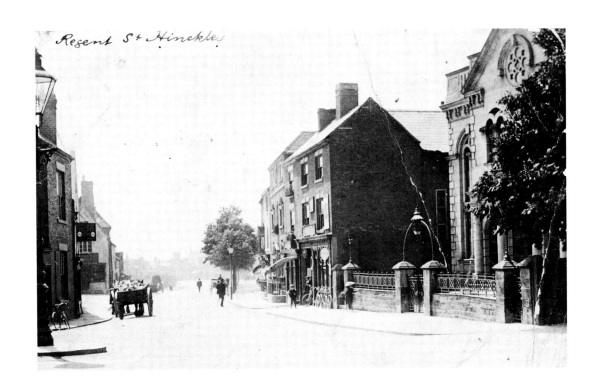

Regent St Hinckley

66. Regent Street in 1903. Many will recognise this photograph because of the façade of the then Congregational Church, which was opened on 25th March 1868. However, few would wish to walk in the middle of Regent Street today!

67. 'Wykes' was the foremost name for many years in Hinckley for good quality fruit and vegetables. This is their shop in Regent Street, opposite the Market Place.

68. Grimm's Lane, 1922. Now renamed as New Buildings. The extended porch, middle right, was soon to disappear as a brick wall and railings were built around the old feoffment cottages. The Drill Hall next to the cottages has seen many uses, from picture palace to do-it-yourself store. The Wesleyan Chapel, mid-left, served a flourishing congregation when it was opened on 7th November 1878. It closed on 12th October 1969 and has since been demolished. The corner shop, so typical of many in the town, retains the same façade and is now a chemist's.

69. The Duke of Rutland pub is still going strong, outliving its neighbouring competitor, the Blue Bell, which was demolished in 1931, to make way for road improvements. Note Marston's 'Dog and Gun'. Along with the 'Union Hotel', just out of sight to the left, the photograph confirms my remark in the introduction about Hinckley's predelection for ale! The paper shop belonging to the Jennings family is prominent on the left. Since then it has been demolished, though the wholesale business remains with the family.

70. Rugby Road, 1925. The front greenery has gone from the Clarendon Road frontage but the building is the same today. Long associated with the Co-op, it is now in private hands. In the background can be seen part of the Gasworks, opened in 1834 and known locally as 'Bleak House'.

71. Lower Bond Street. Bott's hosiery factory is seen clearly in the left background, an early casualty of the dwindling textile output. The house on the corner of Mansion Street, once known as Hog Lane, looks ripe for demolition, as indeed it was, allowing the Liberal Club to be extended.

72. A widened and improved Station Road in the 1920's, with many recognisable and unaltered features here. The corner adjacent to the present Flavell's has been knocked down and is now landscaped as a pleasant garden.

73. Trinity Lane, before slum clearance in 1934. Skep and hamper makers were much in demand by the hosiery industry and small shops abounded wherever there was a need. These cottages were on the left hand side approaching the Coventry Road junction.

74. Queens Park. The new motor pulled mower purchased by the Hinckley Urban District Council about 1930 to keep its parks in trim justified a photograph! Queens Park was once known as Ten Acre Field and was landscaped at the end of the 19th century to celebrate Queen Victoria's long reign. The bandstand appears to be in good order.

75. Leicester Road. If the front of the picture was extended we should see the Grammar School playing fields, now Mount Grace High School. The pavements have obviously not been made up. Note the cumbersome telegraph poles. Leicester Road was then the preserve of the well-to-do and their detached houses.

76. Upper Bond Street showing the site of the Police Station. This photograph was taken in the 1920's when the Manor House had been made into a sanitorium, with no windows. It was eventually demolished so that the present Police Station could take its place.